THE CHOLMLEY HOUSE

This was completed in 1672 by the second Sir Hugh Cholmley, as a new wing to Abbey House. It now houses the Visitor Centre and exhibition.

199 steps leading to Whitby

ST MARY'S CHURCH

The parish church is Romanesque in origin. It includes a gallery, built by the Cholmleys in the early seventeenth century.

Set dramatic... the North... Whitby A... most remarkable... of medieval Eng... king, Oswy, founded a monastery on... mixed community of men and women. It flourished under the rule of St Hild – a noblewoman celebrated for her wisdom and piety – and became a religious centre of the first importance in the Anglo-Saxon world. Numerous prominent figures came to be associated with it and members of its community played a central role in the conversion of England to Christianity.

Oswy's monastery at Whitby appears to have been destroyed by the Danes around 867 and its buildings fell into ruin. But shortly after the Norman Conquest in 1066, Reinfrid, a knight who had fought for William the Conqueror at the Battle of Hastings, visited the headland. The spectacle of the decaying buildings of this celebrated monastery so moved him that he later determined to re-establish the monastic tradition on the site. He returned as a monk in the 1070s and quickly attracted a new community of men. This community followed the Benedictine rule and their monastery, to which the existing ruins on the headland belong, developed into one of the great medieval abbeys of Yorkshire.

In 1539 Whitby Abbey was suppressed by Henry VIII and the buildings were bought by the Cholmleys, a prominent local family. Much of the monastery was then demolished but the abbey church was preserved, possibly as a navigation mark for shipping. Meanwhile the Cholmleys took over the abbot's lodging as a house and parts of this remain in use today. In the 1670s the house was ambitiously remodelled with the addition of a grandly designed new range, which is now the Visitor Centre. This guidebook begins with a tour of this spectacular headland and then a short history of the site and its inhabitants.

TOUR OF
THE ABBEY

The bird's-eye view of the headland on the previous page, along with the plan of the abbey on the inside back cover, should help you to find your way round the site, whether you have entered from the car park to the south or from the town steps and Visitor Centre. The tour goes anti-clockwise round the abbey ruins. The recommended routes are marked in blue and red.

THE EARLY HISTORY OF THE HEADLAND

A vast roofless shell, the ruin of Whitby Abbey is a spectacular sight, visible from miles around. It stands on a massive plateau of rock projecting into the North Sea – one of a series of such geological features along this dramatic, cliff-lined stretch of the Yorkshire coast. The action of the sea has considerably reduced the size of this headland since the Middle Ages, eating away an estimated twenty metres every century. Nevertheless, the plateau is still sufficiently large for the sea to be almost invisible from its centre. In the shelter of the headland to the west is the harbour which has formed the basis of Whitby's prosperity through the centuries.

The precise form and location of the Anglo-Saxon monastery founded by Oswy in 657 on the headland remains a matter for speculation. No traces of its buildings remain visible above ground today and the archaeological exploration of the area has been piecemeal. To complicate matters further, sea erosion and the development of the high medieval abbey may have obliterated much evidence of it. On the basis of evidence from other sites and on literary descriptions, the presumption is that the monastery comprised a cluster of small and irregularly arranged buildings

Opposite: A view of the abbey interior from the west door

Excavations to the south of the abbey between 1999 and 2000 exposed part of a massive cemetery. This was in use during the eighth and ninth centuries and contains more than 1000 graves. The skeletons of men, women and children have been discovered, most of whom appear to have been buried in shrouds. Traces of some wooden coffins have also been found, as well as a handful of other artefacts

including one or more churches within an enclosure. This probably stood in the area of the present ruined church and one part of it – then identified as the nuns' quarters – was excavated in the 1920s. More recent excavations have also revealed a massive Anglo-Saxon cemetery beside the car park to the south of the headland.

 Walk round the outside of the abbey and stop by the information panel overlooking the town and harbour.

THE ANGLO-SAXON MONASTERY

Whatever the precise form and position of the Anglo-Saxon monastery on the headland, its spectacular and exposed location above the North Sea is easy to judge from this spot. The gravestones in the hollow in the ground beside the ruined wall of the nave are the only visible remains of that monastery today. They were excavated from this location during an archaeological dig in the 1920s, which explored this area immediately to the north of the ruined abbey church. Because the excavation techniques used were rather crude by modern standards, the finds of this dig have been the subject of debate ever since. The diggers were

local labourers and they were rewarded for finding things: a shilling in return for a coin and two shillings and sixpence for an unusual or remarkable object.

The original excavators believed that they had found the remains of a stretch of road and a cluster of seventh-century buildings constructed in stone, timber and wattle and daub. These they identified as nuns' quarters on the basis of the brooches, pins and loom weights that they found there. More recently it has been suggested that the supposed road might actually be the footing for an enclosure mound, although there is such a density of Anglo-Saxon finds on the far side of it that this reinterpretation seems questionable. And rather than a cluster of small huts, the excavated foundations have been identified as belonging to a small number of closely built wattle and daub ranges on stone foundations. Cut through the Anglo-Saxon remains in this area were numerous medieval graves, probably all dug from the twelfth century onwards. Whatever the interpretation placed on the excavated remains, there can be no doubt that this was an important site in the seventh and eighth centuries, the home of a wealthy and literate community. The finds included numbers of valuable and remarkable objects. Among them were articles such as binding clasps and styli (writing instruments) which indicated that there were books on the site as well as the implements for writing them. Also discovered was the tombstone of Aelfled, the daughter of Whitby's founder, King Oswy, and an abbess of the monastery.

Above: A photograph of the clearance of the church in the 1920s, showing the excavated remains of the thirteenth-century door between the church and cloister. Notice the depth of rubble which filled the ruined interior of the church

Right: Beside the nave of the church are a number of tombstones, reset in position after they were first exposed in the 1920s. Some are Anglo-Saxon

ARCHAEOLOGICAL FINDS AT WHITBY ABBEY

Martin Allfrey

Excavations at Whitby Abbey have unearthed some of the most important Anglo-Saxon artefacts in England. Although none of the Anglo-Saxon buildings survives above ground, the objects found reveal a thriving community, living, working and worshipping on the headland. The sherds of pottery, animal bones and metalwork – the things which people lost, discarded or in some cases deliberately buried on the headland – help us to build up a picture of everyday life. Finds include decorative objects of silver,

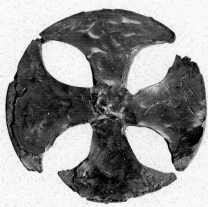

Silver-bronze cross

copper alloy, stone and jet, including book mounts and writing tools, hanging bowls and crosses. Cooking pots and pans, loom weights and spindle whorls, personal items such as combs, pins and strap ends and other everyday items also add to the picture.

Later finds from the medieval abbey help to fill in some of the gaps in our knowledge of the abbey and life within it. The finds include painted glass from the windows, keys from the doors, a balance beam and coins, a jet gaming piece and a carved game board.

From the more recent past we have fragments of pottery and cutlery used by the Cholmley and Strickland families in the eighteenth and nineteenth centuries. Flints from flintlock pistols or shotguns lost while shooting on the headland, wine bottles and clay pipes all tell a different story.

Above: Anglo-Saxon copper alloy stylus, used for writing on wax tablets

Right: Jet gaming piece

Below: Fragment of an eighth-century stone cross with the inscription 'orate pro' ('pray for')

Right: Anglo-Saxon key

Right: Eighteenth-century combined seal ring and pipe tamper

Above: Anglo-Saxon copper alloy pin, used to fasten clothing

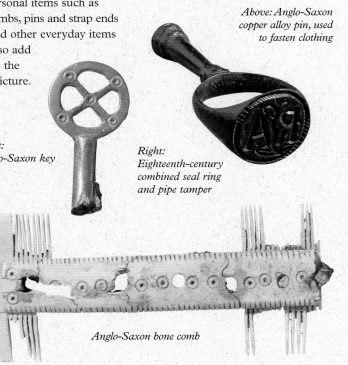

Anglo-Saxon bone comb

Go into the nave of the abbey church and up the two flights of stairs, or ramp, into the magnificent standing remains of the choir.

THE CHOIR OF THE CHURCH

Written into the fabric of the abbey church is a vivid history of the fortunes and aspirations of the Benedictine community that built it, from the eleventh century to the Reformation. The arm of the building in which you are standing served as the liturgical heart of this church, where the monks gathered for Divine Office and the Mass every day.

Traced into the ground around you are the foundation lines of the first known church on the site, which was probably begun in the late eleventh century. This church was cross-shaped in plan, but – as the markings show – terminated at this east end in a series of semicircular apses, a form inspired by eleventh-century architecture in Normandy. Since the community is known to have faced internal divisions and political difficulties immediately after its establishment, this substantial church building is unlikely to have been begun much before 1090.

By the early thirteenth century this Romanesque building was evidently deemed old-fashioned and inadequate. Several great new churches had recently been begun in the area – including those at nearby Byland and Tynemouth – and the monks of Whitby were evidently eager to keep pace with their monastic neighbours and rivals. They responded with a masterful work of early Gothic architecture, closely comparable in design to some of the most ambitious northern buildings of the period, including the choir of Rievaulx Abbey, the transepts of York Minster and the choir of Glasgow Cathedral.

There is no documentary record of the progress of the work to the church, but architectural parallels to other local buildings are so close that we can be fairly certain of the chronology of its construction. Judging from its ornament and form, work probably began on the present choir in the 1220s. This was the first stage in a projected remodelling of the whole building, but initially only the east end of the old church was demolished. The remainder was preserved so that services could continue within the church until the new choir was ready for use. Such piecemeal remodelling of a great church was common in the period.

Above: Isleham Priory, Cambridgeshire, is a rare surviving example of an eleventh-century Benedictine church in England. Although smaller than the contemporary church at Whitby, it still gives a sense of the simplicity of that lost building

Opposite page: Reconstruction drawing of the choir in the fifteenth century, by Judith Dobie

Right: The choir enclosure of the abbey today looking towards the crossing. Traced into the lawn are the foundations of the earlier Romanesque church

Above: The choir of the abbey church, as it is today. The sheer east wall of the church, pierced by ranks of windows, is a distinctively English feature, found in many thirteenth-century buildings in the area

Detail of the carved decoration on the north side of the choir

The south arcade of the choir. The sockets around the arches mark the line of masonry vaulting which has now collapsed

An illustration of c. 1250 showing a cleric, Henry of Chichester, venerating the Virgin and Child. John Brumton's devotion to the Virgin caused him to found his altar at Whitby

JOHN RYLANDS LIBRARY, UNIVERSITY OF MANCHESTER

The choir of Whitby is remarkable for its extraordinary richness. Worked stone was extremely expensive and here every surface dissolves into a profusion of carved detail and moulding. The side walls of the choir are designed with three horizontal bands of arches: an arcade opening into vaulted aisles at ground level; a central gallery storey; and an upper tier of small external windows, called a clerestorey. These bands are arranged in vertical relation to one another and divided by small clusters of shafts to create bays, each one corresponding to an arcade arch. There is no evidence for the seating of a vault in the choir and a curved timber ceiling must have covered the interior. At the east end, the interior is closed by a sheer wall, pierced by three ranks of narrow, arched windows. Irregularities of detail and building levels at the juncture between the east and side walls of the choir suggest that the design of the building was substantially revised during the course of construction.

In the Middle Ages, this splendid interior would have been painted and its windows glazed. Several lost furnishings would also have divided the interior, although few traces of these remain. The focus of the choir would have been the high altar, set on a raised platform towards the east end of the building. Behind this, on the wide step running along the east wall into the aisles, was a series of secondary altars. Lining the sides of the choir towards the west and dividing the aisles from the central space would have been the high-backed wooden stalls for the community.

Go back to the mouth of the choir and stop in the central crossing of the church.

THE TRANSEPTS AND CROSSING

The new choir appears to have been completed by the 1250s, at which time work began on the transepts. Only one of these, the north transept, still stands and it broadly follows the design of the choir with its three-tiered composition of arches and high gable wall. A different kind of stone was used in the work and new forms of architectural decoration appear in it: the lowest level of windows, for example, is richly encrusted with sculpted foliage. Along one side of the transept is a vaulted aisle, which was originally divided into chapels by wooden screens. Sockets for fixing these screens still survive in the masonry, as does a medieval inscription cut into the back of the northern arcade column. This inscription is no longer complete or properly legible, but the original text translates as: 'John of Brumton, sometime servant of God, established at this altar perpetual service to the honour of Blessed Mary.' John Brumton was presumably a monk, but nothing is known about him.

Very little survives of the south transept, which collapsed in 1736. The remains of this building show that it was similar to the north transept, following a mirror-image ground plan and employing a common vocabulary of architectural detail. Unlike the north transept, however, it projected into the built-up space of the monastic cloister. To accommodate the new transept, therefore, it was necessary to jetty it out over the domestic buildings and the staircase visible today beside the church platform was absorbed within the basement of the new structure.

At the juncture of the choir and its transepts a great central tower was also begun. To judge from its details, this was probably completed in the 1280s and survived intact until it collapsed in 1830. With the completion of the tower, work seems to have ground to a complete standstill, probably due to a shortage of funds. The nave of the old church was left standing and the mark of its roof line cut awkwardly into the new tower, as early drawings show. In effect, the church now comprised a massive new east end and a dumpy eleventh-century nave. For the community this disjuncture would not have been a matter of practical importance because it was the choir,

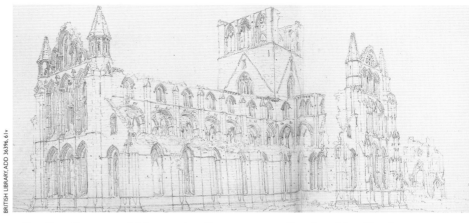

rather than the nave, which served as the operational part of the building. But this unsightly situation was evidently an embarrassment and attempts to complete the church were to continue in fits and starts for at least the next 200 years.

Drawing of the abbey from the north-east in 1811, by J. C. Buckler

View of the crossing and north transept

10

Go back down into the nave and stop when you reach the re-erected column on your right.

THE NAVE

The nave stood largely intact until 1762, but all that now survives of it is this north aisle wall and parts of the west front at the end of the building. When it was complete, the nave was similar in plan to the surviving choir: a central space flanked along its length by vaulted aisles. But the architectural details of the nave were quite different from those of the earlier parts of the church and reflect its confused and long drawn-out construction from around 1260.

Several periods of building are clearly visible in the remains of the nave. The surviving stretch of the north aisle wall, for example, contains two contrasting designs of window, each clearly belonging to a different building phase: three small thirteenth-century windows, and two much larger openings filled with ornate stone tracery patterns. The style of tracery is similar to that in other Yorkshire buildings of around 1300, which suggests that the

Opposite page: This watercolour by J. C. Buckler of around 1811 shows the tower shortly before its collapse. The line of a high gable on each side marks the pitch of a roof. Notice that on the west (left) face of the tower there is also a lower roof line, which probably belonged to the long-serving Romanesque nave

Whitby windows date from the same period. Early drawings also show that the nave was designed with only two tiers of arches – an arcade at ground level and a clerestorey above – rather than three, as occurs in the choir. A surviving section of the arcade shows its details to be of fifteenth-century date.

From the evidence available it is only possible to make educated guesses as to how the nave developed. Most probably, however, the north aisle and west front were constructed by the first half of the fourteenth century around the standing, eleventh-century nave. Work to the west front may have been undertaken in conjunction with an attempt at fundraising for building that was given approval by the archbishop of York in 1334. But this nave was only finally demolished in the fifteenth century, to make way for the rebuilding of the main arcades.

The ground drops away to the south of the nave and the lines of foundations are visible in the grass beyond. You can get a good view of this area either from the edge of the platform on which the nave was built or from the information panel beyond the site of the lost south transept.

The re-erected arcade column in the nave. An inscription records that it was set up in 1790

The surviving section of the nave arcade. This section of the nave collapsed in one piece and has been re-erected. The mouldings of the arches are probably fifteenth-century and contrast to the complex designs of the choir arcade

Juxtaposed details of windows in the north aisle wall: the two designs of window indicate that this wall was built in two stages

THE HIGH MEDIEVAL ABBEY BUILDINGS

Right: Reconstruction drawing of a monk in the warming house

Below: Engraving of the abbey church from the south-west, by the Buck Brothers, 1711. This early view shows the church before either the nave, south transept or the tower collapsed. Note that the two-storey design of the nave, with a ground-level arcade and large windows above, is clearly visible above the aisle wall. The arcaded wall of the ruined twelfth-century Chapter House is also visible beside the standing south transept

Following its refoundation in the late eleventh century, the community at Whitby would have lived in a compact collection of large monastic buildings immediately beside the abbey church. These were enlarged and redeveloped periodically to suit the circumstances and needs of the monks over the next 400 years. Sadly, the monastic buildings have been totally destroyed and we know virtually nothing about them. Nevertheless, there is evidence for the basic layout of Whitby Abbey, and our picture of it can be informed by comparisons with other monasteries.

You are overlooking the former site of the cloister, a large, rectangular courtyard enclosed on each side by a covered walkway. In the late Middle Ages the windows of the cloister walks were colourfully glazed. We know this because

MINDWAVE MEDIA, YORK

the sixteenth-century antiquarian, John Leland, records that one lost stained-glass window here depicted the bizarre subject of William the Conqueror punishing the Scots for their supposed practice of cannibalism.

The cloister served as the hub of the community's daily life and all the principal abbey buildings were arranged immediately around it. Off the east cloister range was the formal meeting chamber of the community, the Chapter House, where business was conducted and daily gatherings held. This was rebuilt at least once during the Middle Ages, by Abbot Richard of Peterborough, who died in 1175. Fragments of the building are visible in an engraving of 1711 by Buck (below). In front of you, to the south, there probably stood the monastic refectory or dining-room. The position of the other rooms around the cloister is less certain, but they must have included a long dormitory chamber in one range and elsewhere a calefactory, a common room heated by a fire. There would also have been an

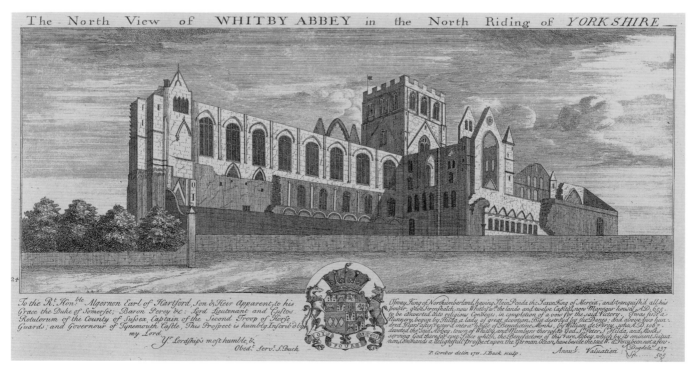

The North View of WHITBY ABBEY in the North Riding of YORKSHIRE

Top: Caedmon House and Abbey Cottage, which possibly incorporate parts of the medieval guesthouse

Above: The exterior of Abbey House from the south-east, with its extension of 1866

infirmary, separate from the abbey cloister, and, by the later Middle Ages, a house for the abbot. Some of this house is probably still encased within the buildings of Abbey House behind the Visitor Centre. Besides these there would have been barns, workshops, storage buildings and a guest-house, remnants of which may survive in the Youth Hostel buildings down the hill to the west of the abbey. Enclosing the entire abbey complex was a high wall entered through a great gatehouse.

THE WEST FRONT

The west front of Whitby was an imposing architectural composition similar in design to that of St Mary's Abbey in York. This was an offspring house of Whitby and one of the richest monasteries in England. The gradual ruin of the façade is well documented in photographs and drawings. In 1914 it was hit by a German shell during the naval bombardment of the town and much of it has been rebuilt.

THE SHELLING OF 1914

THE BUILDER, 28 MARCH 1924/RIBA LIBRARY

A successful raid on Yarmouth by the German navy in the opening months of the First World War had highlighted the weaknesses of British coastal defence. As part of a wider strategy to lure the British High Seas Fleet to destruction another attack was planned. On 16 December 1914 a German raiding force of five battle cruisers and one light cruiser sailed though a gap in the minefields along the east coast near Whitby. There the force divided, one half sailing on to Scarborough, the other to Hartlepool and Whitby. The latter force was engaged by coastal batteries, although it did succeed in shelling Whitby, where some slight damage was done and the west front of the abbey hit. Scarborough was less fortunate and both the town and castle were badly damaged. British public opinion was outraged by these attacks on civilian targets.

Top: This engraving, made by Gibson in 1789, shows the abbey before the collapse of the central tower and west front.

The series of three photographs taken in 1914 shows the final collapse of the west front after the German bombardment. The façade was later rebuilt in its present form, below

Make your way to the information panel overlooking the forecourt of the Cholmley House.

THE CHOLMLEY HOUSE AND COURTYARD

You are overlooking the seventeenth-century forecourt and fine classical façade of the Cholmley range of Abbey House, now the Visitor Centre. In origin, Abbey House was probably the abbot's lodging, a grand residence for the head of the community. Such lodgings were a feature of many great monasteries by the end of the Middle Ages and commonly stood to one side of the monastic complex. After the dissolution of the monastery in 1539, this lodging was taken over by the Cholmley family, who bought the abbey. It has remained in use ever since and has been altered and extended almost beyond recognition as a medieval residence.

The Cholmley House was completed in 1672 by Sir Hugh Cholmley the younger as a new wing to Abbey House and contained all the principal chambers of a fashionable residence of the period. It was arranged on two floors and divided down the centre by a spine wall. It may also have possessed an attic storey. Nothing is known in detail about its internal form or decoration, other than what is implied by the window, door and fireplace openings. Screened off behind it are the earlier buildings, some of them medieval. Sadly, this range was allowed to fall into complete ruin after its roof was damaged during a storm in the 1790s.

The surviving stone shell was repaired after 1866 and further consolidated by the Ministry of Works in 1936. In 2002 English Heritage converted the derelict remains into a Visitor Centre, designed by architects Stanton Williams.

To complement his new building, Sir Hugh also laid out the present cobbled forecourt, which was discovered beneath later layers of surfacing during excavations in 1998. In its original form, the court was encircled by a step-like platform known as an 'alley' built against the perimeter wall. At the same time new terraces may have been laid out to the west of Abbey House, although some of these might also have been created by Sir Hugh's father, who is known to have improved his Whitby residence in the 1630s, repairing buildings and planting the area with trees.

If you came into the site from the car park, don't forget to go into the Visitor Centre and see the exhibition there.

OTHER THINGS TO SEE IN WHITBY

The Whitby Museum in the town also contains numerous artefacts found on the headland and is well worth visiting. So too is the parish church of St Mary just beneath the ruins of the abbey, off the steps from the town. In origin it is a Romanesque building but it has been expanded, refurnished and adapted by every subsequent generation of parishioners and possesses one of the most idiosyncratic and remarkable interiors of any parish church in the country. It includes a gallery, built by the Cholmleys in the early seventeenth century, now known as the Cholmley Pew.

Opposite page: Reconstruction of the forecourt and façade of the Cholmley House. Completed in 1672 this grand façade and forecourt gave a completely new aspect to Abbey House

Left: The 199 steps leading from the town to the abbey

Below left: Although no furniture from the Cholmley House is known to survive, other seventeenth-century pieces, like this table and chair, can give some impression of their probable appearance

Below: The parish church of St Mary, just by the abbey

VICTORIA AND ALBERT MUSEUM

HISTORY OF THE ABBEY

Almost everything we know about the Anglo-Saxon monastery at Whitby and its community is derived from one eighth-century source, *The Ecclesiastical History of the English People*. This text, which can claim to be the first English work of history, was completed in 731 and written by a monk from Jarrow, now in Tyne and Wear – the Venerable Bede. By any standards it is a breathtaking scholarly and literary achievement, presenting a compelling account of the conversion of England to Christianity by a cast of heroic saints and kings. For Bede, the foundation of Whitby was bound up with a turning-point in this history and it figures largely in the narrative he presents.

Bede explains that the place name of Whitby – then known as Streanaeshalch – meant 'the bay of the beacon'. Confusingly, this name cannot be translated as Bede suggests, but there may be a garbled truth in what he writes. Running down the Yorkshire coast at Hartlepool, Huntcliffe, Goldsborough, Ravenscar, Scarborough and Filey was a series of fourth-century Roman signal stations. Could there have been a signal station here too which made Bede explain its name in these terms? No remains of such a structure have been found, but its ruins could easily have been washed into the sea.

Whether or not the Romans were the first to build on the headland, the archaeological and documentary history of Whitby really begins in 657. In that year Abbess Hild established a mixed monastery of men and women here, on the instructions of King Oswy of Northumbria. The idea of a mixed monastery under the rule of an abbess appears to have originated in Gaul, but several other foundations of this kind, such as Ely, Coldingham and Barking, existed in England. These were ruled by women of royal blood, as Hild herself was.

A view by J. M. W. Turner of the town and abbey of Whitby from the south. Turner is one of many romantic artists who have been inspired by the extraordinary setting of Whitby

The thirteenth-century seal of the abbey shows the figure of St Hild with her crozier, a mark of her status as an abbess. To either side are the figures of monks celebrating Mass.

BRITISH LIBRARY, Harl 2908

Pope Gregory sending St Augustine to England to convert the people to Christianity, from a mid-eleventh-century German missal

Far right: An Anglo-Saxon cross shaft from Lindisfarne Priory

Reconstruction drawing of Jarrow in the Anglo-Saxon period

MINDWAVE MEDIA, YORK

Whitby's importance was determined by the political circumstances of Anglo-Saxon England. At this time mainland Britain was not politically unified, but divided into numerous provinces and kingdoms. The borders of these territories shifted continuously according to the fortunes of their respective rulers. It was in this violent and changeable political environment of the late sixth century that two independent campaigns were begun to convert the whole of Britain to Christianity.

The most celebrated of these was initiated by Pope Gregory the Great, who sent an extremely reluctant group of monks from Rome to Britain under the leadership of St Augustine. They landed at Kent in 597 and eventually settled at Canterbury on the site of the present St Augustine's Abbey just outside the city. After a shaky start their work progressed rapidly and in 627 one of their number – Paulinus – baptized the mightiest living ruler in Britain, King Edwin of Northumbria. His kingdom was made up of two provinces – Deira and Bernicia, roughly equivalent today to Yorkshire and Northumberland respectively – but his authority extended north into the lowlands of what is now Scotland and across the whole of England.

Meanwhile, Irish missionaries were at work along the north-western seaboard of Britain. They were led by St Columba, an abbot of outstanding qualities who set up a great monastery on the island of Iona. For both groups of missionaries – both Roman and Ionan Celtic – the work of conversion was intimately bound up with the political relations between different kings and courts and for that reason it was also very dangerous. And while both groups were converting men to the same religion, they cultivated different Christian practices. Notable among these were contrary calendars and fashions of clerical dress. These differences would subsequently become a matter of fierce contention and it was at Whitby that they were eventually brought to resolution.

In 633 the Christian cause in England suffered a devastating setback with the defeat and death of Edwin by the combined forces of a certain King Cadwalla and a pagan nobleman Penda, later king of Mercia, at Hatfield in Yorkshire. Edwin's Northumbrian kingdom was divided and he was succeeded by two kings, Eanfrid and Osric. Both renounced Christianity and the Roman monk

Paulinus, now a bishop, was forced to flee Northumbria. But Cadwalla then also killed both kings, and in 634 Oswald, the brother of Eanfrid, gathered an army to assert his claim to the throne. Oswald had been in exile outside Northumbria for much of his youth and in that time had adopted Celtic Christian practices. When he then successfully defeated Cadwalla, therefore, he turned to Iona for help in re-establishing the church in his kingdom. Under his protection Ionan practices were introduced not only in Northumbria but in certain allied kingdoms as well. Oswald was in turn defeated and killed in 642 by Penda, and it was in direct consequence of this that the monastery at Whitby came into existence.

According to Bede, Penda exploited his victory by devastating Northumbria. Oswald's

successor and brother, Oswy, tried to buy
peace but Penda refused the offering.
In desperation Oswy led a small
Northumbrian army into the field and
pledged both his daughter and the wealth
he had offered Penda to God in hope of
a victory. He was not disappointed. At
the Battle of Winwaed in 655 Penda and
most of his followers, drawn from across
the whole of central Britain, fell beneath
the swords of the Northumbrian army.
The fate of paganism and the future of
Christianity in Britain was sealed.

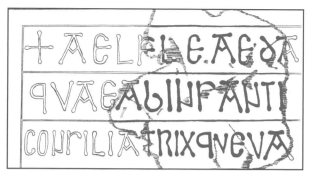

This Anglo-Saxon tombstone
was found at Whitby in the
1920s excavations and is
clearly inscribed on its first
line to Aelfled. It almost
certainly marked the grave of
King Oswy's daughter. It is
one of several pieces of
evidence that point to the
continuity of the monastic site
in this area of the headland

Oswy fulfilled his vow immediately, dedicating
his daughter Aelfled to the monastic life at the
monastery of Hartlepool. This stands about
thirty miles north up the coast from Whitby and
was governed by a certain Abbess Hild. At the
same time he bequeathed twelve parcels of land
to the church. This land was drawn symbolically
in equal portions from the two provinces of
Northumbria, six parcels from Deira and six
from Bernicia. Two years later in 657 Hild
acquired some land at Whitby – possibly one of
these twelve parcels – and set up a new monastery
there, to which she then moved with the princess
Aelfled. These arrangements made Whitby the
royal monastery of Northumbria: it was
endowed with land from Oswy's realm,
associated with his great victory at Winwaed and
served by his immediate family. Its principal
church, dedicated to St Peter, also became the
burial place of Oswy's royal line.

The remarkable figure of Abbess Hild
evidently dominated the new foundation. Bede
describes her as being of noble extraction, like
many notable religious figures of the period.
After living a secular life for thirty-three years she
decided to live in a monastery in Gaul, foreign
exile being a common method of renouncing the
world in this period. But Hild never got to Gaul
and was instead offered a hide of land on the
River Wear in Northumberland by St Aidan, an
Iona-trained bishop. There she lived the
monastic life with a handful of companions.

From the River Wear she moved as abbess
first to the monastery of Hartlepool and then to
Whitby, both of which – Bede tells us – she
governed according to the same rule. What rule
this was is not clear, but given her connections
with St Aidan it seems likely that it was inspired
by Ionan practices. More simply Bede says of it,

'she taught the observance of righteousness,
mercy, purity and other virtues, but especially of
peace and charity. After the example of the
primitive church, no one there was rich, no one
was needy for everything was held in common,
and nothing was considered to be anyone's
personal property.'

Under St Hild's governance Whitby attracted
and fostered a remarkable community. Among
those associated with it were five future bishops,
including St John of Beverley, and the first
known English religious poet, Caedmon. Bede
relates that Caedmon lived for many years
without being able to compose verse. One night
during a feast, the guests were asked in
succession to entertain the company. When the
harp was passed down the table towards him,
therefore, Caedmon retired to the stable, where

MATTHEW POWER

An early fourteenth-century
stained-glass depiction of
St Hild from Christ Church
Cathedral, Oxford. She is
shown as a princess wearing
a crown

Right: Illustration from the Bayeux Tapestry *showing Harold talking with Guy of Ponthieu. The manner in which individuals cut their hair might have been of defining importance even within secular medieval society. Here, for example, the Normans are depicted with the backs of their heads shaven, while the Anglo-Saxons have long hair and moustaches*

Below: The only extant lines of Caedmon's verse are preserved as a quotation in this Anglo-Saxon version of Bede's Ecclesiastical History, *which was produced for King Alfred in the ninth century*

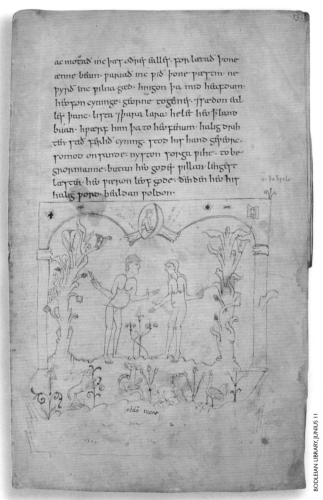

it was his duty that night to look after the beasts. As he slept, he dreamt that a man appeared and called on him to compose verse about Creation. To his amazement he began to sing and compose on this theme spontaneously and when he woke the next morning he completed his poem on the subject. Later he was taken before St Hild and demonstrated his new-found gift. She accepted him as a brother in the community and at her instruction he composed verses in his own English tongue on every kind of religious subject. Sadly, only six lines of his verse, which Bede praises for its exceptional beauty, now survive.

During Hild's rule the monastery was also the meeting place for a church council of enormous subsequent importance. The so-called Synod of Whitby in 664 determined that the Northumbrian church would reject the practices of the Ionan Church and adopt those of the Roman tradition.

Two issues it discussed in this respect were of particular importance. The first concerned the way in which priests cut their hair. Both Celtic and Roman priests had distinctive haircuts or tonsures, the former shaved the front half of their heads and let the remaining hair grow long. In contrast, Roman priests shaved a circle of hair off the top of their heads. A second dispute raged over the calculation of Easter and the Synod's decision on the matter continues to determine the modern calendar.

The feast of Easter falls on a different day each year, its precise timing determined by the cycle of the moon. Each church had developed a slightly different system of calculating the occasion of the feast, with the consequence that they might celebrate Easter up to two weeks apart. King Oswy presided over the Synod and after he had heard the case of each side for their respective calculations of Easter – the Roman tradition of St Peter and the Ionan tradition of St Columba – he posed a question. 'Who', he asked, 'was the gatekeeper of heaven?' 'St Peter', replied the assembled clerics. 'Shall I come to the gates of heaven and be refused admittance by its doorkeeper? No! I will accept the teaching of St Peter and his church and adopt the Roman calendar.' According to one account, written by a priest called Eddius, he delivered this judgement with a smile. Why he might have done so is unfortunately not clear.

The long-term implications of this, and the other decisions of the Synod would be hard to exaggerate. By standardizing the practices of the Northumbrian church according to the Roman tradition, the Synod helped pave the way for the future political unification of England. It also brought all the Anglo-Saxon kingdoms directly within the orbit of the European church, governed from Rome. As we consider the possibility of a politically united Europe, the events of the Synod of Whitby have a particular resonance. The question of the form of a tonsure or the means of calculating a feast were of comparable symbolic and practical importance as, say, the question of the Pound versus the Euro today. And whoever wins these debates will have determined the future of Britain as surely as the triumphant Roman clerics who left Whitby in 664.

St Hild died in 680 at the age of sixty-six after suffering six years of illness and several visions were recorded as marking the event. She was succeeded as abbess of Whitby by Oswy's daughter Aelfled, who ruled the monastery jointly with her widowed mother, Queen Enfled. Both women were remarkable figures. Enfled was a patron of Bishop Wilfrid, the spokesman for the Roman cause at the Synod of 664. Her daughter was active in the politics of the day and there are several stories related about her in a life of St Cuthbert, also written by Bede. She comes across in these as being rather autocratic and determined to get her way. One of her letters also survives, commending a friend to a certain Abbess Adolana of Pfalzel near Treves. Such survivals are a reminder of the internationalism of Anglo-Saxon noble life.

During Aelfled's rule, which lasted until her death in about 714, the monastery acquired the relics of Edwin, the Northumbrian king who had been killed at Hatfield in 633. These relics joined Oswy's remains at Whitby and would have added materially to the prestige of the foundation. The story of their arrival is narrated in the only surviving text associated with the monastery, an anonymous life of Pope Gregory the Great written by a monk in the community between 704 and 714. After the mid-eighth century, the monastery at Whitby disappears from the historical record and it is assumed that it was destroyed by raiding Danes around 867. In this it would have shared in the fate of most of the great monastic houses of Northumbria as the kingdom fragmented and collapsed.

BRITISH LIBRARY, Add 39943 f.1v

St Cuthbert was a leading figure in the Northumbrian church of the seventh century and known personally to Abbess Aelfled. This thirteenth-century illumination shows a monk paying devotion to the saint.

SOCIETY OF ANTIQUARIES, LONDON

Hild, Enfled and Aelfled were not alone among Anglo-Saxon royal women in taking a leading role in the monastic life of the period. This panel from an English altarpiece of c.1425 shows scenes from the life of St Etheldreda, a daughter of one king and wife of another, who founded a double monastery at Ely in 673. The construction of Ely and the death of St Etheldreda are shown in the bottom scenes

LIFE IN THE ABBEY

A Benedictine community, such as existed at Whitby, is composed of a group of men or women living a communal religious life according to the Rule of St Benedict. The Rule was probably written between 530 and 560 by St Benedict of Nursia in Italy. It is a short text, comprising a gently framed series of directions for the life of a monastic community. From its first adoption as the basis for a religious life in the sixth century to the present day, this short text has been observed in a wide variety of ways. It was known in England long before the Conquest, but the Norman observance of it set a new standard of regular monastic life. The monasteries they founded or reformed became known as Benedictine houses and their communities as Black Monks, a name referring to the habits of black cloth that they wore.

In its infancy, Reinfrid's foundation would have observed such elements of the Rule as were practicable for a small number of men living in harsh conditions. But as it grew in size and wealth the Whitby community would rapidly have adopted the complex customs and hierarchy common to all large monasteries of the period. There would have been two sections to the community. A so-called 'novitiate' of young men serving an apprenticeship in the monastic life and a group of choir monks. It was from this latter group of senior monks that all the officers of the monastery were drawn. Most of these had special names relating to their duties, for example the Cellarer who looked after supplies or the Infirmarian, responsible for the infirmary. Choir monks also had a seat in the Chapter House, the formal meeting chamber of the community and a council chamber for debate on matters of business.

The essential features of life within the abbey would have changed very little during the 500 years or so of its existence. The daily timetable, as in a modern abbey, was structured around a series of eight short services comprising readings, psalms and prayers. These are known collectively as Divine Office and would have been sung by the monks in their stalls in the choir of the church. The different offices fell at relatively regular intervals throughout the twenty-four hours of the day, although there were seasonal variations in timing. In order they were Matins, Lauds, Prime, Terce, Sext, Nones, Vespers and Compline. For the night-time offices, the community would have descended to the church directly from their dormitory by the so-called night stair. This probably stood in the lost south transept. But in the day they could enter from the cloister up the surviving day stair.

Besides this daily cycle of the Offices, there would also have been a communal daily Mass in the choir as well as a morning meeting in the Chapter House. Among other things, punishments for breaches of discipline would be carried out at this time. Meals would have been eaten communally in the refectory, but they were eaten in silence to the accompaniment of readings. In their remaining spare time monks might have performed almost any kind of labour, scholarly, contemplative or manual.

Top: Laurence, Prior of the great Benedictine monastery of Durham from 1149–54, at work on one of his histories

Above: A group of Benedictine monks in procession from a fifteenth-century manuscript

Left: Reconstruction drawings of a Benedictine monk shown at table; relieving himself on a latrine; and at work in the herb garden

THE REFOUNDATION OF THE ABBEY

The refoundation of Whitby Abbey was bound up with the sea change in English affairs that followed the Norman Conquest in 1066. In the closing years of the eleventh century the church in England underwent an institutional and architectural revolution. Under the direction of England's conquerors, Anglo-Saxon clerics were ousted from office, monastic practice was reformed and major churches the length and breadth of the country were demolished to make way for vast new Norman buildings. There was also an astonishing expansion in the number of monasteries in England. By 1100, beside the establishment of many new communities to serve cathedrals, nearly eighty new monasteries were founded, of which Whitby was one. These were all Benedictine houses, that is to say governed by the monastic rule of St Benedict of Nursia.

There are several accounts of the re-foundation of Whitby, but the most reliable of these was written in the twelfth century in the surviving benefaction book or cartulary of the abbey. This records that a Norman soldier called Reinfrid, who was in the service of William the Conqueror, turned aside from the route of a journey in the North of England to visit Whitby. He was horrified to see the desolate ruins of this once great monastery and shortly afterwards became a Benedictine monk at Evesham. But rather than settling there he subsequently travelled north with two other monks, Aldwine and Elwine, determined to revive the extinguished tradition of monasticism in Northumbria. They settled first at the ruins of Jarrow, the Venerable Bede's house, but later separated. Reinfrid then moved on to Whitby, where he probably settled in the mid-1070s on the site of Oswy's monastery. It was then described as a cluster of nearly forty oratories, roofless and with their altars exposed to the sky.

Such was Reinfrid's reputation and character that he quickly gathered a group of young men about him, eager to follow a monastic life under his rule. Among them were two figures who were to lead different factions within the community during a complex and momentous crisis in its affairs around 1085. The first was a certain Serlo. He was the brother of a local nobleman called William de Percy, who had originally given Reinfrid the headland site on which to establish his monastery. The second was called Stephen, who probably joined Reinfrid at Whitby in 1078. Unfortunately, there are so many conflicting accounts of what happened that we can only make educated guesses as to the course of events.

The trouble seems to have begun after the death of Reinfrid, who was killed while helping workmen build a bridge probably around 1087. Serlo was elected prior in his stead, but shortly afterwards the monastery suffered a series of raids by pirates and the community was forced to move briefly to Hackness, a short way inland. It seems likely that Stephen contested Serlo's election, because at about the same time he left the community with some of the brethren. He travelled first to the site of the old monastery at Lastingham, but eventually settled at York. There he established the abbey of St Mary's, just outside the city walls, a house that was to grow into one of the richest Benedictine foundations in England.

After bringing the remains of his community back to Whitby, Serlo fell out with his brother William de Percy, the first patron of the monastery. This possibly happened because William wanted to elevate the foundation to the status of an abbey against his brother's wishes. William de Percy may have wanted to do this as an act of devotion marking his departure on Crusade to the Holy Land, where he was later to die. Whatever the case, Serlo then appears to have retired as head of

Benedictine monks saying their office, from a fifteenth-century illuminated manuscript

A fifteenth-century depiction of a construction site. Here labourers work to raise the legendary Tower of Babel

the community and a nephew of his, William, was appointed as the first abbot of Whitby.

We know very little of the early development of the abbey buildings. The discovery of Anglo-Saxon buildings immediately to the north of the present church suggests that the new monastery developed directly on top of its predecessor. Of the process of its construction, however, little is known. The first church, which occupied the same site as the present ruin, is known only from the lines of its foundations. To judge from the form of these and the community's early circumstances, it seems likely that this building was begun around 1090. Beside it there would have developed a collection of monastic buildings arranged around a cloister. These must have been extensively redeveloped over the course of the Middle Ages, but there is one solitary documentary reference to such work: record survives that a certain Abbot Richard of Peterborough rebuilt the Chapter House and was buried within the completed building at his death in 1175.

Despite a destructive sea raid by the king of Norway around 1153 and the excesses of one Abbot Benedict, dismissed in 1148 for squandering the profits of his house, the community at Whitby appears to have prospered throughout the twelfth century. Thanks to generous bequests of land it grew to be one of the richest monasteries in the North-East and supported between thirty and

A winter view of the ruined choir across the so-called abbey pond. Whether this pond really is medieval is not known

forty monks. Of particular benefit financially was the town, whose harbour yielded rich rewards. The abbey struggled hard to exercise complete control over this source of revenue, but not always with success and relations with the town were often strained. It was not until the fourteenth century that the abbey finally quashed the town's claims to independence, securing such rights over it as Plankage, a toll levied on access between the shore and any boat.

By the end of the twelfth century the monastic environment around Whitby changed fundamentally with the arrival of the Cistercians in Yorkshire, a reformed branch of the Benedictine order. The construction of new Cistercian

© TONY BARTHOLOMEW

DRACULA AND WHITBY IN LITERATURE

MARY EVANS PICTURE LIBRARY

Whitby helped provide the inspiration and setting for one of the legends of modern horror fiction. *Dracula* was first published by Bram Stoker in 1897 and several scenes within the novel are set in and around the town. Dracula comes ashore at Whitby in a storm, in the form of a dog, and his first English victim, Lucy Westenra, is attacked on the bench by the church. The abbey does not feature in the novel, although it is described by one of the characters as, 'a most noble ruin, of immense size, and full of beautiful and romantic bits'. Stoker was born in Dublin in

1847 and studied at Trinity College before entering the Civil Service as a junior clerk. In the 1870s he began to enjoy some literary success as a theatre critic and writer of short stories. At the same time he gave up his government work and moved to London, where he helped run the London Lyceum Theatre in partnership with the celebrated

actor Sir Henry Irving. *Dracula* is a typical example of his written work, combining horror and romance. It met with a mixed critical response when it was published and the sinister figure that Stoker created is now most familiar as a cinema image.

Whitby has been a place of inspiration for other writers and artists. Elizabeth Gaskell set her novel *Sylvia's Lovers* in a thinly disguised Whitby during the Napoleonic Wars, and A. S. Byatt's novel *Possession* also features scenes in the town.

Top: Photograph of Bram Stoker

Above: Programme of a stage performance of Dracula, *1897*

Left: Film poster of Dracula, *starring Bela Lugosi*

THE RONALD GRANT ARCHIVE

© SKYSCAN BALLOON PHOTOGRAPHY

Numerous Cistercian houses were founded in Yorkshire in the twelfth century. Rievaulx was one of the most successful of these. The choir of this church was rebuilt in the thirteenth century and compares closely with that at Whitby

PUBLIC RECORD OFFICE

Henry VIII, as depicted in the initial of the Valor Ecclesiasticus, *a survey of monastic property on the eve of the Dissolution*

buildings in the locality such as at Byland and Rievaulx and the redevelopment of other great monastic churches in the North prompted the monks of Whitby to begin the rebuilding of their own church in the 1220s. After the completion of the choir and transepts over a period of about sixty years, the work languished. This was probably due to the crippling expense of the project and in 1320 a surviving disciplinary inspection of the abbey reported that the community was desperately in debt. Shortly afterwards in 1334 the Archbishop of York gave his formal consent to a fundraising campaign by a senior monk, John Lumby, to help complete work to the church. He was to go on a tour in order to meet and encourage individuals, or institutions, to give money towards the project. Even so, the nave was probably only finally completed in the late fifteenth century.

Little is known of the day-to-day existence of the community. The disciplinary visitation of 1320 indicates that at that date hunting for pleasure by the community had become a problem: the

monks were forbidden to shoot with bows and arrows and it was instructed that no dogs be kept within the precinct. It goes on to direct that should any dogs be found they were to be soundly beaten and expelled. There are also a few surviving account rolls from the monastery in the 1390s but they record little of general interest.

The last abbot of Whitby was a certain William Davell, who surrendered the abbey to Henry VIII's commissioners on 14 December 1539. At that time the community was twenty-two strong and the monastic estates had the annual value of £437 2s 9d. This revenue made Whitby a very wealthy foundation locally, but it is interesting to note that it is also one of the lowest incomes of any independent Benedictine house in England.

ABBEY HOUSE AND THE CHOLMLEY FAMILY

On 1 March 1540, three months after the surrender of the abbey, the precinct and its buildings were leased out to a certain Richard Cholmley of Kingthorpe, near Pickering. Known as 'the great blacke knight of the North', Sir Richard was a successful soldier against the Scots and built up a substantial estate during the Dissolution. Later in his lifetime he bought the freehold of the site and it descended to his son, Francis, who remodelled the old abbot's lodging and used it as his house. What happened to the remaining domestic abbey buildings is not known,

This drawing by Wenceslas Hollar is one of a series of scenes showing the English colony of Tangiers in the 1670s. The younger Sir Hugh worked on the great wall, or harbour mole (left) and a settlement called Whitby grew up on the shore beside it, used by labourers brought from his home town in Yorkshire

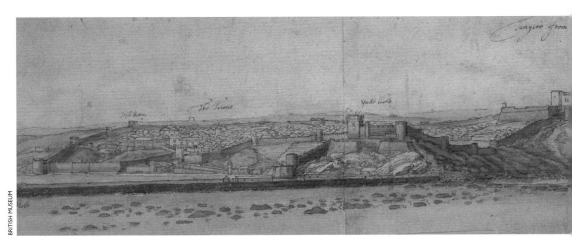

BRITISH MUSEUM

THE MEMOIRS OF
SIR HUGH CHOLMLEY, 1600–57

The history of the Cholmleys and their relationship to Whitby is documented in an extraordinary collection of papers written by Sir Hugh Cholmley between 1648 and his death in 1657. An important figure in Yorkshire, Sir Hugh produced three so-called *Memorials* describing events in the Civil War, among them an account of his defence of Scarborough Castle in 1645. They are a gripping read – action-packed narratives of politics, battles and intrigue.

After his wife's death in 1655, Sir Hugh also began work on a set of memoirs. These comprise not only an account of his own life, but also a history of the Cholmley family from the reign of Henry VIII. They chart the family's rise to prominence in Yorkshire in the wake of the Dissolution of the Monasteries and the subsequent squandering of the family fortune by Sir Hugh's father and grandfather. The memoirs focus, however, on the events of Sir Hugh's own life. After a turbulent youth he

PRIVATE COLLECTION

Portrait of Sir Hugh Cholmley, depicted as a commander in full armour, c. 1640

proved adept at managing his estates and succeeded in paying off the debts he inherited. Writing of his life in Abbey House before the troubles of the Civil War, he reminisced that he had, 'lived in as handsome and plentiful a fashion at home as any gentleman of my rank in all the country; I had between thirty and

forty in my ordinary family, a chaplain who said prayers every morning at six, and again before dinner and supper; a porter who merely attended the gates which were ever shut up before dinner when the bell rung to prayers and not opened till one o'clock, except for some strangers who came to dinner, which was ever fit to receive three or four beside my family without any trouble: and what ever their fare was they were sure to have hearty welcome. Twice a week a certain number of old people, widows or indigent persons, were served at my gates with bread and good pottage made of beef, which I mention that those who succeed may follow the example.'

Sir Hugh's son, another Sir Hugh (1632–89), also wrote the beginnings of his own memoirs as well as several accounts of incidents in his life. This combined collection of family papers is an invaluable source for the history of Whitby and offers many fascinating insights into seventeenth-century life in England.

*Right: Walcot Hall,
Cambridgeshire, was also
built by Sir Hugh Cholmley
between 1674–8 and shows
some similarities to the
Whitby range*

*Opposite page: Reconstruction
drawing of the interior of the
Cholmley House*

*Below: A reconstruction
drawing of the Cholmley
House by Judith Dobie, as it
was first completed in 1672.
The existence of dormer
windows in the roof and the
design of the principal
windows is inferred from
other buildings of the period*

but nearly all trace of them had disappeared before 1700 and they have never been fully excavated. In the meantime the church was stripped of lead, but left intact as a standing shell. Two big collapses – the fall of the nave in 1762 and that of the tower in 1830 – have left the building in its present state.

Abbey House probably underwent little further change until the 1630s, when Sir Hugh Cholmley the elder improved the property, enlarging the number of its buildings and replanting the grounds around it. Sir Hugh later played a prominent role in the Civil War in Yorkshire, fighting first for Parliament and then for the King as commander of the garrison at Scarborough Castle. The events of Sir Hugh's life are colourfully recorded in the memoirs that he wrote and we know from these that the house at Whitby was pillaged during the fighting and garrisoned until after the fall of Scarborough. Sir Hugh was also important in developing the town of Whitby, building a mole in the harbour and setting up alum works to exploit the natural deposits of this material in the locality. This industry was already profitably established at Whitby, and Sir Hugh must have realised how much he stood to gain from it.

The next important series of changes to the house were completed in 1672 at the direction of Cholmley's son, also called Hugh. He built an imposing new range in the classical style across the front of the older buildings of Abbey House (now the Visitor Centre). This is one of two fine surviving houses he erected for himself in England. (The other is Walcot Hall, near Peterborough.) It seems likely that the grounds around the house were extensively re-landscaped at this time and the present entrance forecourt laid out. Sir Hugh spent considerable time in the English colony of Tangier between 1663 and 1674, where he worked as resident engineer overseeing the construction of a great harbour

mole. This project, which was eventually abandoned, was of unprecedented ambition and one of the wonders of seventeenth-century civil engineering.

During the eighteenth century Abbey House remained in use but the range added by Sir Hugh Cholmley fell into decay after the loss of its roof in the early 1790s. The decay was only arrested after the property had come into the possession of the Strickland family, whose descendants still own the house. In 1866 W. C. Strickland substantially enlarged the residential parts of Abbey House and shortly afterwards consolidated the ruins of the Cholmley range by the insertion

MINDWAVE MEDIA, YORK

JUDITH DOBIE

CAPTAIN COOK

BRIDGEMAN ART LIBRARY/NATIONAL MARITIME MUSEUM, LONDON

Among the most celebrated figures associated with Whitby is the navigator, cartographer and sea captain James Cook. Born at Marton in Cleveland, Yorkshire in 1728, Cook first came to Whitby to serve an apprenticeship in a general store in the town. At the age of eighteen he became apprentice to a substantial Whitby ship owner and three years later was rated able seaman in his master's collier-barks, vessels used in North Sea trade. Rather than pursue this career, however, he volunteered for the Royal Navy and advanced rapidly through its ranks. In 1768, after demonstrating his exceptional abilities as a surveyor, he was appointed to command a scientific expedition to the Pacific. This was the first of three major expeditions he undertook, each of which he sailed in Whitby-built ships. Aside from his achievements in charting the Pacific, South Atlantic, Arctic and Antarctic oceans, he also solved the problem of scurvy among seamen. He was killed in 1779 at the age of fifty in the Hawaiian Islands during a dispute with Polynesian natives over the theft of a cutter.

Above: Portrait of Captain Cook, by Nathaniel Dance, c.1800

Left: The Captain Cook monument in the harbour at Whitby, erected in 1912

*View of Whitby from the
headland*

of bracing arches within the shell of the building. These were removed in 1936 after the Ministry of Works took on responsibility for this part of the house.

In 1920 the family handed over the abbey ruins to the Ministry of Works, who subsequently cleared the ruins and excavated the area beneath and around the church. The abbey ruins and the Cholmley range both came into the care of English Heritage in 1984. It later commissioned the architects Stanton Williams to design a new

Visitor Centre inside the Cholmley range of Abbey House and this work was completed in 2002. This is part of a wider project undertaken in conjunction with the Strickland Constable Estate and Scarborough Borough Council to conserve the site and improve visitor access. The work has included the creation of a new car park, thereby assisting in the conservation of fragile remains; excavation in advance of cliff collapse; and conservation of boundary walls on the headland.

WHITBY AND ITS INDUSTRIES

Since the Middle Ages the wealth of Whitby has been derived largely from the sea and in particular from the large, seasonal catches of herring which can be made along this stretch of the coast. During the nineteenth century the town also briefly developed into an important whaling centre. But the locality of Whitby is also rich in mineral resources and at certain periods these have been successfully exploited. In the seventeenth century the Cholmley family consolidated its fortune by working the natural alum deposits along the cliffs. Alum was used in the process of tanning leather and for its qualities as a mordant, a substance that fixes dyes. During the mid-

nineteenth century there was also a very successful jet industry at Whitby. Jet is a black fossilised wood that can be intricately carved and highly polished, properties which have long made it popular for trinkets. Whitby possesses some of the finest deposits of jet anywhere in the world and around 1800

a naval pensioner, Captain Tremlett, pioneered a process of turning beads in the material. With the aid of this technology and helped by the attention of the royal family, carved Whitby jet became immensely fashionable over the course of the nineteenth century. The fortunes of the industry peaked in the 1870s when some 1400 men and boys were employed working jet. But the boom was short-lived and by the 1930s the market and industry had dwindled almost to nothing.

Above left: Jet watch chain and hair comb, made at Whitby

Left: Jet workers at Whitby in Victorian times

Below: The harbour at Whitby, photographed in 1880 by Frank Meadow Sutcliffe. The abbey and headland are in the background

View of the headland and abbey from across the harbour and the River Esk

FURTHER READING

Bede, *The Ecclesiastical History of the English People*, trans. L. Sherley-Price and revised by R. E. Latham, Penguin Classics, 1990

Burton, J., *The Monastic Order in Yorkshire, 1069–1215*, Cambridge University Press, 1999

Cartularium Abbathiae de Whiteby, J. C. Atkinson (ed.), Surtees Society, lxix (1879) and lxxii (1881)

Hawkes, J. and Mills, S. (eds), *Northumbria's Golden Age*, Sutton, 1999

Lawrence, C. H., *Medieval Monasticism*, 3rd edn, Longman, 2001

Memoirs and Memorials of Sir Hugh Cholmley of Whitby, 1600–57, J. Binns (ed.), the Boydell Press, 2000 (Yorkshire Archaeological Society Record Society, cliii, 1997–8)

Peers, C. and Radford, C. A. R., 'The Saxon Monastery at Whitby', *Archaeologia*, Vol. lxxxix (1943), pp.27–88

Victoria County History, North Riding of Yorkshire, Vol. II